D0988829

Julie Moos: Hat Ladies

by

Robert Hobbs

Foreword by

Elias Hendricks, Jr.

Birmingham Museum of Art

Published by

Birmingham Museum of Art

2000 Eighth Avenue North

Birmingham, Alabama 35203-2278

www.artsbma.org

In conjunction with the exhibition

Julie Moos: Hat Ladies

Birmingham Museum of Art

May 26 – August 11, 2002

Copyright ©2002

Birmingham Museum of Art

Foreword: Hat Sisters

© Elias Hendricks, Jr.

"I Got Freedom over My Head": Julie Moos'

Hat Ladies of New Pilgrim Baptist Church

© Robert Hobbs

All rights reserved.

No part of this book may be reproduced or used in any

form, or by any means—graphic, electronic, or mechanical,

including photocopying, recording, or taping—without

the written permission of the publisher.

ISBN 0-931394-49-X

Cover

Hat Ladies (Mrs. Rose and Mrs. Pleasant)

2000/2001

C-print, Edition of 5

40 x 52 inches

Design

Jean Crutchfield

Color

dPimaging, David Ridderhof

Printer

Progress Printing, Richmond, VA

Hat Ladies, 2000/2001

C-prints, Editions of 5

40 x 52 inches each

Julie Moos dedicates this catalogue to David

Acknowledgments

The first time I saw the series of photographs called the *Hat Ladies,* I was immediately impressed with the dignity and beauty of the sitters and the transcendent quality of the images themselves. Julie Moos began photographing the women of New Pilgrim Baptist Church after an introduction by Elias Hendricks, a member of the church, patron of the arts and former Museum trustee, who wanted to honor and celebrate the lives of these women – both for their style and for the roles they play in defining and supporting their community. Julie came to the project as an outsider, a Canadian/New Yorker who has lived in Birmingham for only a few years. She approached her subjects with respect and distance, and she structured the photos using the formal devices from an earlier portrait series. She used soft natural lighting together with a strobe and a neutral backdrop and paired most of the women to create double portraits. The emphasis for the women was the attire, most importantly, their hats, but the photographs are about more than style. The photographs give us a sense of rich tradition and pride in a community that has established its place in local history. In his foreword, Elias refers to the women as the "Hat Sisters." Importantly, when the series was finished, Julie named it the "Hat Ladies." The slight separation implied by this title change reflects the objectivity as well as the respect with which the artist approached the subject, and the works stand out because they record, not just the details of dress, but the details of lives.

I would like to thank the people who made this project a reality: Elias and Gaynell Hendricks, for inspiring and supporting the work; the Reverend Nelson H. Smith, Jr., of New Pilgrim Baptist Church; Carol Williams, the church secretary who helped Julie set up a studio in the church; and Ida Bryant, the Hat Lady who was instrumental in organizing the photo sessions. Funding for the catalogue has been generously provided by the Birmingham Art and Cultural Commission, Jack Drake, and Michael Nesbitt. For the exhibition, we are grateful to our local lenders: Dr. Alain Bouchard and Dr. Karin Straaton, Jack Drake, Elias and Gaynell Hendricks, Scott and Kelly Miller, Jim Sokol and Whatley Drake LLC. Other lenders are Ira Statfeld and Michael Recanati, New York, and Refco Group, Ltd., Chicago.

My thanks also to Fredericks Freiser Gallery in New York, for all of the assistance they have provided with organization of the exhibition; The Lab, Birmingham; to Robert Hobbs, the Rhoda Thalhimer Chair of Art History, Virginia Commonwealth University, who provided an eloquent and scholarly essay that places the work in a broader context; to Jean Crutchfield, for her talents as the catalogue designer; and Suzanne Voce Stephens, who curated the exhibition for the Museum.

Gail Andrews Trechsel
The R. Hugh Daniel Director
Birmingham Museum of Art

Foreword: Hat Sisters

Elias Hendricks, Jr.

I first met Julie Moos at a cocktail party, hosted by a local patron of the arts. Julie and her husband, David, had just moved here from New York. I started teasing them about how slow everything was in Birmingham.

We walked slower, talked a lot slower and went to bed a lot earlier down here. My wife and I had moved here from New Jersey some years before and I assured her that even as a returning Southerner it took some getting used to.

During the course of the evening we started talking about the differences between Southerners and Northerners. So, after we fought the Civil War all over again (Southerners love to do that), we settled on the topic of Southern uniqueness.

"First shoes," I told Julie, "Look around, just at feet." Most of the women that were Southern had something different working on those shoes – a bow, a flap of leather, jewelry, something – not a plain shoe could be found. The only plain shoes, upon further investigation, belonged to the women born and raised in the North.

My wife, a Southern, shoe lady, tried to defend all Southern women by dismissing my observations as craziness. "But I saved the best for last," I spoke up, "HATS." Southern women single-handedly saved the hat industry from oblivion. Nobody does hats like Southern women, and nobody but nobody does hats like the women in my church – New Pilgrim Baptist Church.

In our church we have a group of ladies we call the Hat Sisters. These ladies believe that a woman is not dressed to go to church without a matching hat. It's a dying art form. These ladies have a style and flair found nowhere else.

Every Sunday they are immaculately groomed and sartorially correct. Dresses, shoes, jewelry all matching, and on top, creations you wouldn't believe. Turbans, feathers, glitter, flowers, all matter of things affixed to these hats and sprinkled across the sanctuary so that it becomes a sensual feast for the eyes. A lot of women try hats, but some are masters; the masters of the art form In my church earn the name of HAT SISTER. Style all their own, all over the top, but in good taste. It's really something to see, something to experience.

I've been trying to interest local photographers in capturing this uniquely Southern phenomenon. Every one of them thinks it's no big deal. I think it needs to be celebrated.

When I saw an exhibition of Julie's photographs at The Altamont School, I knew she would be perfect for this project. The next time I saw Julie I invited her to photograph the hat sisters. Julie said she was interested.

I truly didn't believe she was serious; I really thought she was just humoring a nice old man who was talking her head off. Some time later Julie called and said she was ready to go to church.

Men's Day was always a day when the Hat Sisters showed up from other churches. It was a duel to see who was the sharpest. Of course, the ladies of my church defended their turf, and the battle of the Hat Sisters was on. I chose such an occasion to invite Julie to New Pilgrim Baptist Church.

That Sunday we met at the Church and we sat Julie in the middle of the sanctuary. I pointed out the reigning divas of hatdom. Mrs. Carr, who used to sell hats, was a city-wide style leader. Our team anchored by our leader Ida Bryant, whose tall stateliness was the perfect background for the more elaborate chapeau. I pointed out other members of our home team that had staked out their territories all over the sanctuary; Mrs. McKinstry, Mrs. Dudley and Mrs. Bryant anchored the front. Mrs. Carr came in with her entourage and took center seats to challenge. But at 11:45 the doors opened and Ms. Pleasant stole the show with a feathered creation that was like no other.

Julie watched all this and was fascinated by what she saw. By now I realized that Julie was from "really up North," all the way to Canada. I also had come to realize that she was no ordinary local photographer. So, to my dreams of documenting a cultural phenomenon that I thought was a dying art form, the Lord had sent a world-class photographer who could look at it with clear and unbiased eyes. She could record and also celebrate Southern Sunday Dressing through the eyes of a true artist.

Congregation at the New Pilgrim Baptist Church, Birmingham, Alabama.
(Photograph by Leon Mickens)

Thank you, Julie, for letting the world see the strength, beauty, style, grace, dignity and pride in Sunday Dressing at New Pilgrim Baptist Church, Birmingham, Alabama, interpreted by the masters – The Hat Sisters.

Elias Hendricks, Jr.
Member of New Pilgrim Baptist Church

P.S. We also have great church services. This is just the icing on our spiritual cake.

New Pilgrim Baptist Church, Birmingham, Alabama. (Photograph by Leon Mickens)

"I Got Freedom over My Head": Julie Moos' Hat Ladies of New Pilgrim Baptist Church

Robert Hobbs

Miracle Sunday, Birmingham, Alabama: May 5, 1963

At 4 p.m. that Sunday, after a morning of integrating white churches, the crowd of faithful gathered for a prayer meeting at Nelson Smith's New Pilgrim Baptist Church. . . . At around six o'clock, a group estimated at between one thousand and three thousand left the church and walked west into the setting sun on Sixth Avenue. . . . This was the largest demonstration of the campaign so far, and proof that the children had finally gotten their parents behind the Movement. . . .The men and women proceeded, singing "I Want Jesus to Walk with Me." Spectators jamming the porches of neighboring houses were hushed in contrast to past onlookers. When the first marchers reached the police barricade two blocks from the jailhouse, they knelt and began to pray, as their wake of churchpeople billowed to the ground. Flanked by firemen, Captain Glenn Evans ordered them to disperse.

Billups [Smith's co-pastor] stood and looked into the nozzles of the hoses, "We're not turning back," he said. "We haven't done anything wrong. All we want is our freedom. How do you feel doing these things?" Then he began to chant, "Turn on your water, turn loose your dogs, we will stand here till we die." Tears streamed down his face. The crowd chimed in, a chorus swelled.

As with most miracles, the particulars of that Sunday are difficult to document, especially since reporters were among the white people Connor [Birmingham's Public Safety Commissioner] had barred from the scene. What the press did observe from a distance was that the demonstrators retreated across the street. . . where they prayed and sang for half an hour, with water guns trained on them.

Movement participants would swear that Connor barked at his firemen, "Turn on the hoses," and the firemen had just stood there. "Dammit?" Connor said, "Turn on the hoses." But the firemen fell back. Nelson Smith believed they had caught the marchers' "spiritual intoxication." Some firemen were crying, and one was heard to say, "We're here to put out fires, not people." Connor would insist that the firemen were simply being considerate of the marchers' Sunday clothes. But most of the Negroes felt what Smith called "the hand of God" as never before, as they arose from their prayers singing "I Got Freedom over My Head" and strode through a line of policemen and firemen parting like the Red Sea.

Diane McWhorter, *Carry Me Home*, 2001

The series of eighteen pieces of photo-based art comprising *Hat Ladies* (2000-2001) represents collaborations between Julie Moos and her subjects, members of the historically important New Pilgrim Baptist Church. Because Moos has chosen to reaffirm in these images her sitters' elaborate art of self-presentation, including their most tangible symbols of the freedom over their heads, I will look first at their ongoing practices before considering the artist's contributions.

Hat Ladies, Birmingham, Alabama: October-November, 2000

The senior sisters of Birmingham, Alabama's New Pilgrim Baptist Church, located in the African American community of Ensley, are called "the hat sisters or ladies" in deference to their stunning crowns of fur, felt, and straw. These special creations are customarily adorned with festoons of feathers, cascades of artificial flowers, or bold assemblies of sequins and rhinestones. The regal headdresses attest to the churchgoers' desire to glorify their heavenly Savior each Sunday by outfitting themselves in the most splendid possible raiment. Although their numbers account for only about five percent of New Pilgrim's entire congregation of thirteen hundred members, the hat ladies – a self-selected group whose bid to membership is ratified by their decision to wear sumptuous headgear – are conspicuously present in the congregation each Sunday. One member of this informal club, in particular, Mrs. Pleasant, is gently ribbed by her peers for being "Missy Eleven-Thirty" because she provides a distinct focal point to this special assembly's requisite pageantry by making a dramatic entrance a full half-hour after service has begun.

Now the oldest generation of a rapidly disappearing matriarchal culture, the hat ladies of New Pilgrim are particularly noteworthy representatives of a country-wide African American phenomenon. The ones seen in Julie Moos' photographs are mostly retired service industry workers who have been employed as nurses, domestics, and sales clerks in stores appealing mainly to black customers. Fiercely proud, many of them have earned the long-term respect of their fellow parishioners for decades of good deeds that include supporting the church, looking after the sick, and raising money for college scholarships. Some of them participated in the passage of meaningful Civil Rights legislation in the 1960s by helping to initiate a decade earlier the registration of black voters. At the height of the Civil Rights movement, they were in their twenties, thirties, and forties, and thus intimately involved in many events crucial to its success, so that the final song of thanks and victory on what came to be known as Miracle Sunday, "I Got Freedom over My Head," would even today assume a special spiritual and political resonance for them when they choose their Sunday dress. It is this historical background in relation to the hat lady phenomenon that Julie Moos set out to represent in *Hat Ladies*. At New Pilgrim the senior sisters form a formidable chorus of unwavering righteousness as they visibly uphold the policies and admonitions of their famous Civil Rights-era minister, Reverend Nelson H. Smith, Jr., the former secretary of the revolutionary Alabama Christian Movement for Human Rights (ACMHR), who was nicknamed "Fireball" because of his rousing sermons and fierce oratory. In the annals of the Civil Rights movement, he is credited with saying before Miracle Sunday, when the prospect of integration seemed hopeless, the following words of encouragement: "It's dark in Birmingham now and it's going to get darker, but when it is the darkest that's when you can see the stars of freedom."[1] As their contribution to millennial events, the senior sisters assisted members of the congregation in organizing a 47th year celebration of Rev. Smith's pastorship. At the same time that they honored Rev. Smith, Jr., they paid homage to New Pilgrim's position as a center for the Civil Rights movement.

The senior sisters' hats are showy and intentionally expensive. Often they are priced at several hundred dollars apiece, with fur hats costing as much as six hundred dollars apiece. They might be seen as their generation's equivalent to the current New York City penchant for shoes, particularly designs by Prada and Manolo Blahnik that are equally expensive and that have similarly inspired collections numbering from dozens to even hundreds of examples. Designed primarily for an African American clientele, the churchgoers' hats, which are often unique, can be found in a number of Birmingham stores: the specialty shop called "Fifth Avenue Hats" is a favorite place, and Cotton's Department Store in Ensley is another. From time to time Cotton's will feature trunk showings by such popular New York designers as George Zamau'l, who sells hats for two hundred dollars and up, wholesale. It is a common practice for the senior sisters to place expensive items in lay away for months, sometimes even a couple of years, and pay for them in installments. Not content with a special hat for each season, many church ladies have succumbed over the years to the temptation of collecting great numbers of these creations so that their Sundays become fashion opportunities for modeling new designs and bringing special reserved treasures out of storage. One of the hat ladies, Mrs. Carr, who sold hats for Cotton's, has assembled a collection of over 300 such items that she lovingly and meticulously curates, storing them carefully in their original boxes that adorn shelf after shelf in her home. These collections often represent a life-time of collecting.

Choosing a creation to wear on a particular Sunday is a serious and concerted undertaking for Mrs. Carr and other members of her group. It involves taking into consideration the total outfit, the season, the known hats of other senior sisters, as well as the dresser's own spiritual mood. Dressing for church is not only an occasion, it is also a theatrical event and a moment of grace in which the very real issues of old age, diminishing resources, and concerns about family members are briefly put aside. Mrs. Bryant has described in poignant detail the tremendous boost she receives each week when she dresses for church. Because she suffers from a number of health problems, Mrs. Bryant often wonders if she is even able to participate in services. But once she decides on a hat, coordinates it with a compatible outfit, and makes herself up, she begins to feel well enough to complete her ensemble by slipping on three-inch heels.[2]

Such an emphasis on hats indicates their preeminent role in a fluid economy of signs communicating power and prestige. While the unwritten and constantly changing interactions of a specific community of hat ladies help to define the dynamic relationships of the members constituting it, thus necessitating an intense and long-term investigation, we might consider a few overarching rules regarding hats that the New Pilgrim and other groups of hat ladies observe. The hat must be acquired by its wearer and not be a hand-me-down, except under the most extreme circumstances when it is inherited from a beloved friend and worn in their memory. It must never be loaned out. Since it is the most visible testament to one's individuality, it must, if possible, be unique. In addition, the hat should be worn with a special panache attesting to the innate stylishness of its owner, even to the point of turning it around so that the back becomes the front. Or it is shown off with a distinctive tilt – a "hattitude" – for which its owner becomes known. Rather than being equated with only one style of hat, a senior sister reaps enormous cultural capital by demonstrating her ability to carry off, with seemingly effortless aplomb, radically different styles.[3]

Julie Moos' Photographs

Although Julie Moos knew neither of these elaborate proscriptions and prescriptions nor the highly elaborate rituals of the hat ladies of New Pilgrim, she was definitely intrigued when Elias Hendricks – a member of New Pilgrim and a recently elected Birmingham city councilman – invited her to photograph the senior sisters of the New Pilgrim Baptist Church. She remembers that he wanted her to make a historical record of them, something that could be shown at the Smithsonian Institution. Mr. Hendricks' invitation was based on his familiarity with Moos' previous work, particularly the project that she had completed in 1999 of a private school in Birmingham titled *Friends and Enemies*. The idea of photographing high school students came to Moos when the school's headmaster, Martin Hames, asked Moos to mount an exhibition at The Altamont School's Cabaniss Fine Arts Center, a noted Birmingham venue for the display of regional art. With images of the tragic massacre of twelve students and one teacher at Columbine High School in Colorado in April, 1999, still very much on Moos' mind, she decided at Altamont to underscore the types of intense relationships and non-relationships that can develop among teenagers in one high school. She set up her studio in an unused classroom and photographed pairs of students who were either close friends or not at all connected with one another.

For this series, Moos combined the two very different genres of fine art portrait photography and documentary work that could be said to be equal claimants to different periods of her own artistic development. The fine art photographs relate to her undergraduate years at McGill University when she was an English major, and the documentary aspect is an outgrowth of her studies in the School of Journalism at New York University, before turning to photography at the International Center of Photography. In each of her images of Altamont's senior class a forceful gap separates two classmates who gaze directly in front of them and not at the camera – similar to the experience of posing for a driver's license photograph. And yet the overall effect is far different from the snapshots found on these official forms, since Moos generously empowers the presence of each of the figures through her use of a large-format camera and production of the photographic image on a large scale. Obviously intrigued by the mixture of telling observation and impressive individuality seen with objectivity and directness that characterizes each of Moos' images, Hendricks thought her approach might be an appropriate way to honor New Pilgrim's hat ladies.

After accepting Hendricks' offer to introduce her to this congregation where the proposal to photograph the hat ladies was immediately endorsed with enthusiasm, Moos faced the important decision of when to initiate the project. Although she was urged by New Pilgrim parishioners to focus on either the Christmas or Easter season when special regalia would be worn, she thought that less thematic attire would be more characteristic of the hat-lady phenomenon and provide a more convincing image of it. For this reason she decided to work during the months of October and November and to set up an impromptu studio in the hallway outside the sanctuary. She depended on Mrs. Bryant and the serendipity of whoever would show up, thus leaving open to chance and to the senior sisters themselves which individuals would become pairs. Throughout this eight-week period, Moos photographed hat ladies both before and after the church service, which is scheduled between 11:00 A.M. and 1:30 P.M. During service she sat with the congregation. Thirty-one hat ladies agreed to be photographed in pairs with the exception of Mrs. Bonner, who wanted to be presented alone, and Mrs. Lewis, who was worried about getting a ride home and could not wait for a partner. Mrs. Dudley, Mrs. McKinstry, and Mrs. Taylor whose hats and outfits make them appear to be completely different people, were each photographed on two different Sundays.

After studying the eighteen images making up Moos' series, one might ask why the senior sisters' styles seem so eloquently "period." Do the styles of the hat ladies refer back to the youth of their owners? Do they reflect an era of unassailable glamour when hats were still considered de rigueur by broad sectors of the population? Is glamour itself now a mid-twentieth-century phenomenon that can be only conjured up through knowing references to the past? What exactly is the relationship between this finery and the Civil Rights era? Are the senior sisters claiming a grandeur that was denied to them in the past?

Julie Moos reports that during her photographing sessions her subjects would mention the names of Jackie O, Marilyn, Hillary Clinton, and Princess Di, whom they revere. After looking at these photographs reflecting both the hat ladies' wonderful art of self-presentation and Moos' austere and affective records of them, I think about how they would enjoy attending a garden party for British gentry where their own sense of high style together with their stately decorum would be on a par with the finery and presence of the other ladies there.

In these photographs, Moos enters into an elaborate and subtle game of self-deception and revelation, a polite conspiracy between photographer and her subject in which she reveals their masks as masks, and they in turn revel in them. What is presented in these eighteen images is a screen – the grand opera of the southern Baptist African American faith that is both sacred and secular. Moos both supports and undermines the stage on which these mostly retired blue- and pink-collar workers act out imposing and benign scenarios. Instead of looking behind masks for an underlying reality, Moos conveys the cogency and effectiveness of personae that reveal the aspirations and needs of an upwardly mobile and totally worthy constituency.

But Moos doubles these images and then multiplies them by a factor of eighteen. The majesty of each figure is challenged by the adjacency of its peer since the partner's appearance reveals the elaborate masquerade that the two are indeed constructing. One hat lady connotes individuality; two imply a collaboration, and a series of pairs indicates an ongoing practice that superintends all its adherents, making them subscribers to a specific cultural norm, a set of known rituals. Only one of Moos' sitters, Mrs. Bonner, figured out the transformation that doubling entails and tried to obviate it by requesting a solitary sitting, but the poignancy of her missing partner in the unoccupied space to her left compromises her splendid isolation by directing attention away from her and in the direction of the ongoing cultural convention of hat ladies to which she belongs.

In these photographs there is a poetic rhyming with the genre of passport photography that Moos' one-time hero, the German photographer Thomas Ruff, initiated. References to passport photography implies that the sitter has been granted full rights to the great American dream. This dream includes an attendant license to participate fully in the unbridled consumerism for which this country has become renowned and the hat ladies are now becoming known. Yet if Moos' portraits take their cue from the frontality and apparent neutrality of the passport image, her work undermines that authority through the assertion of pairing. For Moos, individuality is only obtained through interaction. In the case of these images it is twofold, since there is an implicit connection between the two sisters as well as their connection with Moos herself.

An important subtext that separates these sitters from English gentry is the pan-African invocation of crowns suggested by their hats. Although none of the examples in Moos' series conjure up images of turbans and head wraps, such inspirations do appear at New Pilgrim during Black History Month when church members celebrate their roots through dressing in dashikis and head wraps that bespeak a symbolic homecoming. Their ongoing celebration of elaborate and even wonderfully excessive array of designs has no doubt been justified in terms of its ability to connect present-day wearers with imagined prototypes. It is a dream that designers, manufacturers, and retailers have all capitalized upon. Although none of New Pilgrim's senior sisters in Moos' photographs are wearing

dashikis or felt chapeau that directly copy regal tribal crowns, there are a number of imaginative hybrids that indirectly allude to an imposing African lineage, such as Mrs. McKinstry's dark headdress with ostrich feathers as well as her white one with flowers, Mrs. Merritt's flanged turban with a bronze bow, Mrs. Rose's tilted crown, Mrs. Taylor's crenelated structure reminiscent of Dogon architecture, and Mrs. Arnold's comely turban. In addition, the leopard patterns found in Mrs. Lowe's and Mrs. Brown's hats, scarf, and collar as well as the zebra prints in Mrs. Carr's suit and Mrs. Dudley's hat are telling signs of their family's atavistic place of origin. As Felecia McMillan, the parishioner of another southern church, pointed out:

The more I study Africa, the more I see that African Americans do very African things without even knowing it. Adorning the head is one of those things, whether it's the intricate braids or the distinct hairstyles or the beautiful hats we wear on Sundays. We just know inside that we're queens. And these are the crowns we wear.[4]

In many hats found in Moos' photographs, then, we can detect evidence of a concerted desire on the part of some senior sisters to use dress as a symbolic medium that is capable of bearing witness to their heritage and distant roots.

But the situation is even more complex than the pan-African strain suggests since not all the sitters in Moos' random sampling of the hat ladies' collections choose to affirm their ancestral heritage through their dress. Some, in fact, look less to Africa and more to Hollywood, where the prototype for Mrs. Bryant's dramatic fur chapeau appears to be a 1940s movie about the gilded age, while

Mrs. White's seems to echo the roaring '20s. There is certainly a great deal of Edith Head and Bob Mackie in the minds of some of the designers and their colluding patrons who have entered into a wonderful conspiracy whereby period glamour is re-construed as a timeless and universal realm.

The prevalence of black and white is an ongoing thematic in Moos' entire assembly of portraits. Its frequency makes one wonder if the colors are intended not only as fashion statements but also as symbolic references to ameliorated race relations. In other words, it makes one think that the combination of black and white might be a way for these survivors of unchecked racism to embody physically their long-term desire for complete integration with full and equal rights.

In thinking about the role of Moos' photography it is tempting to recall the late nineteenth- and early-twentieth-century photographer Edward Curtis. Recently scholars and theorists have taken Curtis to task for playing to the expectations of racial stereotyping when he portrayed Native Americans in their rarely worn traditional dress, transporting them momentarily from the constant deprivations of reservation life they were suffering to a mythic and even dreamlike halcyon realm predating the advent of the white man. Believing in the inevitable demise of Native Americans who would either be assimilated into the mainstream or disappear, Curtis fed the unquenchable nostalgia of a generation responsible for perpetuating these ills, a generation which apparently wished to avoid the dire conclusions of their policies and rhapsodize instead about the lost grandeur of a passing people. Critics continue to have problems with Curtis, his misplaced nostalgia, and his ideological delusions, and their lack of tolerance is an instructive counterpoint for our analysis of Julie Moos' photographs since she avoids so

many of the traps in which Curtis' work is ensnared. Working a century later than Curtis, Moos has entered into a full collaboration with the hat ladies. She has created straightforward and unblinking views of an upwardly mobile African American middle class indulging itself in the obvious material benefits of the American dream while finding ways to symbolize through their dress their African roots and aspirations for a more fully integrated world through their hats, their literal representations of the song "I Got Freedom over My Head." Although the photographs are definitely Moos' creations, the hat ladies self-presentation through their dress constitutes their own estimable aesthetic contribution to these works. The two have come together to create a remarkable series of collaborative pieces that reaffirm life as a creative and highly meaningful theatrical performance that we all tacitly agree to orchestrate and then ratify as reality.

Notes

[1] Diane McWhorter, *Carry Me Home: Birmingham, Alabama, The Climactic Battle of the Civil Rights Revolution* (New York: Simon & Schuster, 2001), p. 335.

[2] Julie Moos, telephone conversation with author, 2 February 2002. This and other statements attributed to the artist in this essay are taken from this extended telephone conversation.

[3] Michael Cunningham and Craig Marberry, *Crowns: Portraits of Black Women in Church Hats* (New York: Doubleday, 2000). Although these rules are not specified as rules per se, their frequency among the many interviews making up the text of this book strongly supports my claim that they in fact constitute a set of rigidly adhered-to African American assumptions about the etiquette of owning and wearing hats.

[4] Ibid, p. 187.

Mrs. Merritt and Mrs. Crum

Mrs. Foreman and Mrs. Daniels

Mrs. Taylor and Mrs. Bryant

Mrs. Taylor and Mrs. Poole

Mrs. Mason and Mrs. Levison

Mrs. Lowe and Mrs. Brown

Mrs. Bonner

Mrs. Huntley and Mrs. McKinstry

Mrs. Goodwin and Mrs. Taylor

Mrs. Rose and Mrs. Pleasant

Mrs. Lewis

Mrs. Dudley and Mrs. Hall

Mrs. McKinstry and Mrs. Williams

Mrs. Arnold and Mrs. Davis

Mrs. Watkins and Mrs. Craig

Mrs. Dudley and Mrs. White

Mrs. Carr and Mrs. Thornton

Ms. Maiden and Mrs. Maiden

Julie Moos

Born November 25, 1965, Ottawa, Canada

Lives and works in Birmingham, Alabama

International Center of Photography, New York, NY, 1992

M.A., New York University, New York, NY, 1991

Sorbonne University, Paris, France, 1989

B.A., McGill University, Montreal, Canada, 1987

Awards

2001   Artist-in-Residence, Contemporary Art Museum St. Louis,
St. Louis, MO

Solo Exhibitions

2002   *Hat Ladies*, Birmingham Museum of Art, Birmingham, AL

2001   *Domestic*, Fredericks Freiser Gallery, New York, NY

2000   *Friends and Enemies*, Fredericks Freiser Gallery, New York, NY
1 PLUS 1, The Altamont School, Cabaniss Fine Arts Center,
Birmingham, AL

1999   *Or Never Remembered*, Clayton Staples Gallery, Wichita State
University, Wichita, KS

Selected Group Exhibitions

2002   Whitney Biennial 2002, Whitney Museum of American Art,
New York, NY

Girls, Georgia State University School of Art and Design,
Atlanta, GA

Curator's Forum: Collecting Contemporary Art, Ackland Art Museum,
The University of North Carolina at Chapel Hill, Chapel Hill, NC

Staging: Janieta Eyre, Julie Moos, Zwelethu Mthethwa,
Contemporary Art Museum St. Louis, St. Louis, MO

2001   *New Acquisitions*, Johnson County Community College,
Overland Park, KS

Chelsea Rising, Contemporary Art Center, New Orleans, LA

Full Frontal, Jan Weiner Gallery, Kansas City, MO

2000   *Collectors Choice*, Exit Art, New York, NY

Fay Gold Gallery, Atlanta, GA

1999   Three-person exhibition, Sable-Castelli Gallery, Toronto, Canada

1998   *Interior Space*, Erman B. White Gallery of Art, Butler College,
El Dorado, KS

1997   *Tiny Works*, Project Gallery, Wichita, KS

1996   Saks Fifth Avenue Windows, New York, NY

Selected Biography

2002   Hobbs, Robert. *Julie Moos: Hat Ladies*. Exhibition catalogue.
Birmingham, AL: Birmingham Museum of Art.

Longshore, Jane. "In The Vicinity: Exhibitionism." *Black & White*,
17 January, p. 9 (with illustration).

Odita, Odili Donald. "Review: Julie Moos, Fredericks Freiser." *FlashArt*,
January/February, p. 94 (with illustration).

"Whitney Biennial 2002: The List." *Flash Art*, January/February, p. 37
(with illustration).

2001   Bookhardt, D. Eric. "Reviews: Southeast, New Orleans." *Art Papers*,
September/October, pp. 38-39.

"Goings On About Town," *The New Yorker*, 19 November, p. 22.

Kinzer, Stephen. "Enron's Fall Reverberates In the Houston
Arts World." *The New York Times*, 18 December, p. E1.

Rubin, David. *Chelsea Rising*. Exhibition catalogue. New Orleans, LA:
Contemporary Arts Center, March-June, pp. 19, 34 (with illustration).

Thorson, Alice. "Challenging Beauty." *The Kansas City Star*, 13 April,
p. 28 (with illustration).

Weigand, Susan. "Photography and the Human." *Review*, April, p. 40
(with illustration).

Yablonsky, Linda. "Downtown Armory: Surviving the Growing Pains."
Art & Auction, April, p. 74.

2000   Coman, Victoria. "Facing the Future, Altamont Pupils Pair up for Photo
Exhibit." *The Birmingham News*, 12 January, p. S1 (with illustration).

"Good Morning Alabama." Fox 6 News. Interview by Jermelle Pruitt,
5 January.

Johnson, Ken. "Friends and Enemies at Fredericks Freiser." *The New
York Times*, 6 October, p. E40.

Longshore, Jane. "In The Vicinity: Exhibitionism." *Black & White*,
6 January, p. 8 (with illustration).

McAuliffe, Michael. "Collector's Choice." Reviewny.com,15 December.

1999   MacKay, Gillian. "Lacquered Labels, Found Photos, Terrifying Tots."
The Globe and Mail, 27 February, p. C11.

1998   Norman, Bud. "From Behind the Photographer's Eye." *The Wichita
Eagle*, 15 March, p. D1 (with illustration).

1997   Holman, Rhonda. "Examining the Spaces Within." *The Wichita Eagle*,
9 November, p. D1.

Public Collections

Ackland Art Museum, The University of North Carolina
at Chapel Hill, Chapel Hill, NC

Birmingham Museum of Art, Birmingham, AL

Enron Corporation, Houston, TX

The Hallmark Photographic Collection, Kansas City, MO

Johnson County Community College, Overland Park, KS

Groupe L'hoist, Paris, France

Neuberger Berman, New York, NY

Refco Group, Ltd., New York, NY and Chicago, IL

Sprint, Overland Park, KS

Unus Foundation, Birmingham, AL

Wake Forest University, Winston-Salem, NC

Julie Moos is represented by Fredericks Freiser Gallery, New York, NY.

Elias Hendricks, Jr.

Elias Hendricks, Jr. was elected to the Birmingham City Council in November 2001. A former executive for BellSouth, Hendricks combined business experience with entrepreneurial spirit to build one of the premier pre-school child-care businesses in the Southeast. Hendricks received a B.A. degree in History and Psychology from Clark College in Atlanta, a Master's degree in African History from the University of Ghana in West Africa, and a Master's of Business Administration from Pace University in New York. Hendricks has served on a variety of civic and cultural boards including the Birmingham Museum of Art, Opera Birmingham, The Birmingham Civil Rights Institute and Operation New Birmingham. Elias and his wife Gaynell have one son and two daughters.

Robert Hobbs

Robert Hobbs holds the Rhoda Thalhimer Endowed Chair of Art History at Virginia Commonwealth University. Author of 20 books including monographs on Edward Hopper and Andres Serrano, he has curated more than forty major exhibitions that have been presented in ten countries. Among them are: *Abstract Expressionism: The Formative Years*, which was shown at the Whitney Museum of American Art, and *Robert Smithson: Sculpture*, which was also presented at the Whitney Museum of American Art and subsequently was selected to be the official U.S. representation at the 1982 Venice Biennale. In 1996 he curated *Souls Grown Deep: African-American Vernacular Art of the South* for the Summer Olympics in Atlanta, Georgia. Other recent touring exhibitions include the Lee Krasner retrospective, which concluded its U.S. tour at the Brooklyn Museum of Art in 2000, and *Milton Avery: The Late Paintings*, which completes its U.S. tour in 2002. Currently he is completing a major monograph on Alice Aycock and curating an exhibition of Anselm Kiefer's monumental woodcuts for the Trust for Museum Exhibitions, Washington, D.C. His latest endeavour is serving as U.S. commissioner for the 2002 São Paulo Bienal where he is presenting the work of Kara Walker.